BOOK ANALYSIS

By Cassandra Gibbons

Cat's Eye

BY MARGARET ATWOOD

Bright
≡Summaries.com

MARGARET ATWOOD   9

CAT'S EYE   13

SUMMARY   17

Childhood
Adolescence
Adulthood

CHARACTER STUDY   27

Elaine
Cordelia
Grace
Elaine's mother
Jon
Josef

ANALYSIS   35

Friendship and bullying
Memory
Chronology and perspective

FURTHER REFLECTION   43

FURTHER READING   47

MARGARET ATWOOD

CANADIAN NOVELIST

- **Born in Ottawa in 1939.**
- **Notable works:**
  - *The Handmaid's Tale* (1985), dystopian novel
  - *Alias Grace* (1996), historical novel
  - *Hag-Seed* (2016), a novel retelling Shakespeare's *The Tempest*

Margaret Atwood is a Canadian novelist who was born in 1939 in Ottawa. She grew up one of three children and moved around a lot because of her father's job as an entomologist. She did not attend school full time until she was 12, but spent much of her childhood voraciously reading. After graduating from the University of Toronto, majoring in English, she achieved an MA from Harvard University. She has one adult daughter and has been in a relationship with another novelist, Graeme Gibson, since the 1970s.

Atwood's oeuvre spans genres and literary mediums: she is an accomplished writer of novels, short fiction, poetry and non-fiction. She is best known for her 1985 novel, *The Handmaid's Tale*, which is classed as one of the best examples of dystopian fiction from the 20th century alongside the likes of Orwell's *1984*, although Atwood herself prefers the term 'speculative fiction' to describe the novel. Atwood has won a slew of literary prizes over her long career, including the 2000 Man Booker Prize for her novel *The Blind Assassin*.

CAT'S EYE

A REFLECTIVE NOVEL

- **Genre:** modern fiction
- **Reference edition:** Atwood, M. (1988) *Cat's Eye*. London: Little, Brown.
- **1st edition:** 1988
- **Themes:** friendship, bullying, art, memory, sexual difference, religion

Cat's Eye was published in 1988, three years after the publication of *The Handmaid's Tale*, and was shortlisted for the Man Booker Prize and for the 1988 Governor General's Award. It is perhaps the most autobiographical of all of Atwood's fiction, as the protagonist shares many traits with Atwood herself, notably an entomologist father. The novel is set in roughly the same era as its publication date, and is told largely in flashback, interspersed with present-day chapters. For purposes of clarity, the below summary is told broadly in chronological order.

The novel tells the story of Elaine, a successful painter, who reflects on her life and in particular on her childhood friendships after she returns to Toronto, the city in which much of her childhood took place. As a young child she was badly bullied by three friends, and this bullying has affected her entire life, particularly in relation to her relationships with women. The experience has also affected her art, which is ultimately the reason for her return to her hometown: she is being celebrated in a Toronto-based retrospective show.

SUMMARY

CHILDHOOD

Elaine Risley is a Vancouver-based painter who is returning to Toronto, where she spent much of her early life, to attend a retrospective show in her honour. She begins to reminisce about her childhood, and particularly her childhood friend Cordelia, with whom she has lost touch. She thinks back to her early childhood, when she did not go to school but rather travelled around with her family because of her father's job as an entomologist. She dreamed of having female friends her own age, but came to regret this when her three friends, Cordelia, Carol and Grace, began to bully her.

Elaine was happy to be invited to go to church with Grace and her family, but overheard Grace's mother saying to her relative that Elaine deserved the bullying she got from the other girls because she came from a non-religious family. Elaine was teased by her friends when she did well in school, and then teased by them for doing badly (which she did on purpose after being teased for being clever). Cordelia often talked about Elaine in the third person as if she was not there and talked to Grace and Carol about improving her behaviour. They banished Elaine from bedrooms and sitting spaces at school and told her to think about what she had said wrong.

Two events particularly traumatised Elaine. Once, Cordelia dug a hole in her back garden and made Elaine sit in it with the entrance covered. On another occasion, Cordelia threw Elaine's hat down into a ravine and made her go and get it. When Elaine fell through the ice her friends abandoned her, and she made it home half frozen after imagining the figure of the Virgin Mary guiding her. Her mother had been suspecting bullying but had done very little about it. Elaine's attempts to stay at home were stymied when her friends politely asked her mother if Elaine could play with them. Elaine was miserable during this period and picked the skin off her feet until they bled. She was forced to give up her job babysitting a neighbour's son out of fear that her friends would hurt the baby.

Cordelia apologised to Elaine over the phone for leaving her in the ravine. Elaine suspected that this apology was forced out of her and worried about the retribution she would face for this later. When Cordelia casually mentioned punishing Elaine for telling on them – which Elaine denied – Elaine somehow found the strength to sever ties with her so-called friends. She resisted their attempts to win her back with kindness and stopped going to church with Grace and her family. She knew that they simply wanted someone to bully, and was angry with herself for not stopping it sooner.

ADOLESCENCE

Elaine was able to make normal, nice friends after her experiences with Grace, Cordelia and Carol, who all went to different schools. When Elaine came to start high school, however, her mother received a phone call from Cordelia's mother. Cordelia's mother was hoping the girls could walk to school together, as Cordelia was in fact expelled from her private school and would now be going to the same school as Elaine. Elaine agreed to this despite her mother's worries, and the pair reconnected in high school. The relationship dynamic between the two changed, as Elaine began to hold power over Cordelia. She could tell Cordelia to do things and be obeyed, and even had the power to scare Cordelia, by, for example, telling her that she, Elaine, was a vampire.

Elaine, and the wider community, was troubled during this period by the murder of a girl down in the ravine. Elaine helped Cordelia with her schoolwork, particularly by dissecting her worm and frog for her in biology lessons, but Cordelia proved to be more interested in the performing arts and performed poorly in her academic work. When Cordelia reminisced about their childhood together, glossing over her relentless bullying of Elaine, Elaine struggled to deal with it. She slowly stopped seeing Cordelia, despite vague promises to keep in touch with her. She also decided, in the middle of her biology exam, that she wanted to be a painter.

Present-day Elaine wonders when her memory will begin to fade as she looks back to her student days. She studied Art and Archaeology at the University of Toronto and also took life drawing classes at Art College taught by an Eastern

European man called Josef Hrbik. She would go to bars with her male classmates and Josef because she could, as a woman, get them into mixed sex areas of the bar. Josef, who had struck up a relationship with one of Elaine's classmates, Susie, soon struck up a relationship with her too. Elaine and Susie essentially shared Josef.

Cordelia got back in touch with Elaine around this time, and was in a much better place than in high school. Elaine went to see her in a play but was unable to identify her friend because of the costumes. Susie ended her relationship with Josef after nearly dying from complications following a botched attempt at inducing her own abortion. Elaine also ended her relationship with him shortly after this, unable to cope with the pressure of being his sole girlfriend. She instead began to date a classmate, Jon, although he determinedly kept their relationship casual and open.

ADULTHOOD

After university Elaine found moderate success as an illustrator of book covers. She and Jon got married after an unplanned pregnancy. Elaine was too scared to have an abortion after witnessing Susie nearly die. By the time their daughter, Sarah, was a toddler, their marriage was in trouble and Elaine realised that Jon was having an affair. Elaine began to get involved with women's groups and even put her art into a women's only exhibition. Ink was thrown over one of her works by a religious zealot whom she first confused with her childhood friend, Grace. Elaine moved to Vancouver with her daughter when her marriage to Jon finally ended, where she continued to find success and also married her second husband, Ben, with whom she had her second daughter, Anne.

Elaine's brother, Stephen, died when his plane was hijacked and he was shot. Elaine's parents never quite got over his death. Elaine helped her mother go through some old things after the death of her father and found the cat's eye marble she had so treasured as a girl. The last time she saw Cordelia was when her old friend asked her to come and see her in an institution. Cordelia was committed to this institution after turning to pills and asked Elaine for help in escaping. Elaine refused and tried to move on, but was never able to get over her connection with

Cordelia. As a parent she frequently worried if her daughters were being subjected to bullying, or if they were bullying themselves.

In present-day Toronto, Elaine is staying at her ex-husband Jon's apartment while in town for the retrospective. She marvels at how different the city is compared to her memories. She gives an interview in which she needles the interviewer and is consequently written about in a disparaging way. She is touched by the affection of Charna, who is working on the retrospective, but put off when a young admirer talks about how Elaine's work captures an era. This makes her feel old and historical. She does not especially want the retrospective, but feels that it would be ungrateful to turn it down, particularly when taking into consideration how few women painters get retrospectives.

Elaine expects Cordelia to show up to the retrospective but she does not. Elaine is unsure whether she wants Cordelia to turn up or not. She worries about their old friendship and if she was too mean to Cordelia in high school, and comes to the conclusion that her old friend is likely dead. She has sex with her ex-husband

and plans to flirt with men at the retrospective. On her way home afterwards, she is sat next to two older women who are gossiping happily together. Elaine realises that she does not miss Cordelia, but rather she has missed the opportunity to have a good friendship with a woman. In realising this, she manages to find some closure.

CHARACTER STUDY

ELAINE

Elaine is the protagonist of the novel. The novel begins with her thinking about her childhood friend, Cordelia, and wondering what her life is like now that they have lost touch. She is visiting Toronto, where she spent a significant part of her childhood and adolescence, because her paintings are being honoured in a retrospective. For Elaine, however, the important retrospective does not solely concern her work, but her life. As she explores Toronto she thinks back to her childhood, and how her relationship with Cordelia affected her life. It has affected her parenting style, as she often frets about her own daughters' friendships, and it also affects her painting. The most recent pieces in the retrospective depict the incident in which Cordelia threw her hat into the ravine and made her go and fetch it.

Another way in which Cordelia's bullying has affected Elaine's life is her ability to form female friendships. Her relationships with women, such as fellow mothers in Vancouver, or the feminist collective in Toronto, have never gone beyond skin-deep friendships. Elaine's trust in women was irreparably damaged by her experiences of bullying. She was horrified, for example, when her parents suggested that she might try and take an entrance exam for a more prestigious, single-sex high school. She has always had an indelible sense that men have been her allies, even though some of the men in her life have betrayed her and tried to control her. Elaine is a thoughtful character, but she is not above being cruel herself: on the occasions when Cordelia decides to taunt Carol instead of her, she is quick to join in. She also teases Cordelia when they are teenagers and the power balance in their relationship swings towards Elaine.

CORDELIA

Cordelia plays the role of both tormentor and victim in the novel. During her childhood she bullies Elaine to such an extent that Elaine hopes to get ill in order to avoid spending time with her friends. She isolates Elaine, teases her and tells her how to behave. This is all done under the pretext of Cordelia helping Elaine to improve herself. She punishes Elaine and encourages their other friends to report back to her about Elaine's behaviour. Carol can do this because she is in the same class as Elaine, and Grace monitors Elaine when they are at church and Sunday school together. Whatever Elaine does, she is punished by Cordelia and the others.

Cordelia is portrayed as devious and clever. Few adults suspect her bullying nature because she has perfected a polite tone of voice in which to address people and manages to charm them. Her power begins to wane as she hits adolescence, however, and her academic struggles threaten her position in high school. She tries to compensate for this by throwing herself into theatre productions and also by talking about rude things in order to maintain her status. By the end of high school she needs Elaine but is rejected, and her life begins a downward spiral that ends up with her being institutionalised. Her fate is unclear, but her overall impact on the events of the novel is immense.

GRACE

Grace is part of Elaine's friendship group and bullies her alongside Cordelia and Carol. Elaine is an object of fun for Grace and her friends: they amuse themselves by making tormenting her their project. Grace and her family are very religious and Grace invites Elaine to go with her and her family to church and Sunday school. Despite Elaine making a good effort at Sunday school, Grace and her mother seem to think that she deserves punishment for not having been raised a Christian. Grace is portrayed as rather a petulant child: when she is playing with Carol and Elaine and they want to play something different to what she wants to do, she claims to have a headache and sends them home. She uses her popularity to play her friends off against each other. Her religious mother is the subject of several of Elaine's paintings.

ELAINE'S MOTHER

Elaine's mother is occupied as a housewife and looks after her husband and two children, as well as their house and garden. She is a kind woman but does not initially notice that her daughter is being bullied. When she begins to suspect, her inaction continues, and she fails to notice that Elaine helps her at home because she wants to avoid her friends. When Elaine's friends ask her mother directly if she can play with them, Elaine's mother unwittingly destroys her daughter's excuse and condemns her to further bullying. Years later, she assumes that the bullying was all done by Carol and Grace, failing to spot the major culprit. She is presented as a nice but ineffective character.

JON

Jon is Elaine's first husband and the father of her first daughter, Sarah. When their relationship begins Jon continues to see other women, and he is unfaithful to Elaine when they are married. Their marriage is a result of their unplanned pregnancy and they are ill-suited as a couple. Jon is quietly dismissive of Elaine's art, particularly in relation to the show she puts on with her friends from the feminist collective. Despite their incompatibility as a couple, Jon and Elaine are drawn to each other and forgive each other the violence and lies that plagued their marriage. When Elaine comes back to Toronto she stays in Jon's apartment (while he, for the most part, stays elsewhere) and they have dinner together. They end up reconnecting both as friends and also on a sexual level.

JOSEF

Josef Hrbik is the teacher of a life drawing class attended by Elaine. He continually shows a lack of respect towards women, from touching the female model used in the life drawing class to rearrange her hair and posture, to his attempts to mould Elaine into the perfect girlfriend (by telling her what she should wear). He uses his influence as a teacher to have sexual relationships with both Susie and Elaine, both young students, but clearly feels that he has no responsibility towards them. Elaine thinks to herself as an adult that she would be horrified if either of her daughters were in a similar relationship with a man like Josef. Josef has the effect of making Jon look like a much better partner for Elaine in comparison, although in reality neither is the right partner for her.

ANALYSIS

FRIENDSHIP AND BULLYING

The most prominent relationship of the novel –
that of Elaine and Cordelia – is defined by its love/
hate dynamic (although Elaine herself is wary of
the word hate). Elaine feels a platonic chemistry
between the pair when they first meet:

> "This time her voice is confiding, as if she's talk-
> ing about something intimate that only she and I
> know about and agree on. She creates a circle of
> two, takes me in." (pp. 78-79)

The depiction of the relationship between
Elaine and Cordelia is designed to show that
relationships can be far from simple. Elaine's
feelings about Cordelia are often confused and
contradictory. Despite Cordelia's treatment of
her (and that of Carol and Grace), it takes Elaine
a long time to stop considering them to be her
friends. Before she and her family moved back to
Toronto, she craved female friendship because
it was something she had never experienced.

Her lack of experience results in her classing her appalling treatment as normal, and something to be endured.

While Elaine does find the strength to end her poisonous friendships with Cordelia (temporarily) and Carol and Grace (permanently), she never quite manages to categorise their behaviour as hateful. She denies ever having hated Cordelia and continues having a friendship with her throughout high school despite the lack of affection between them. She sums up her conflicted feelings early on in the novel:

> "Hatred would have been easier. With hatred, I would have known what to do. Hatred is clear, metallic, one-handed, unwavering; unlike love." (p. 136)

Elaine would be forgiven by most readers for turning to hatred after she is dehumanised at the hands of Cordelia. A particularly chilling example of this dehumanisation is Cordelia's use of the third person to refer to Elaine in front of her when discussing how she and Carol and Grace should punish her. In doing so she strips Elaine of her agency and treats her little better than a dog in need of training. When Cordelia and Elaine reignite their friendship in high school, Elaine is careful to not let history repeat itself. The shift in the power dynamic between them is evidence that there is strength in numbers, as Cordelia clearly does not feel able to subdue Elaine in the same way without backup from Carol and Grace. Cordelia is in a weakened position due to her expulsion from her private school and Elaine has learned how to use her quick wit to put people down. This rather mean streak of defensiveness in Elaine is quite possibly a coping mechanism developed to protect herself from further bullying. As she associates friends with bullying, she is quick to warn people off becoming her friend, which, in her mind, should stop them bullying her. Her inability to separate friends from bullies stops her from developing meaningful relationships with women for the rest of her life.

MEMORY

The telling of the story relies on memory, both that of Elaine and that of Atwood herself. Even if the novel is not as autobiographical as it may appear, Atwood did draw on her memories at the very least for the historical, geographical and social setting of the novel. Social movements like feminism, and art movements particular to the time, are all represented. The historical elements of the novel are particularly vivid. They depict a Canada valuing a close relationship to British culture, which is evident in the songs that are sung in schools (*God Save the King* and *Rule Britannia)* and the close following of the fortunes of the Princess (and later Queen) Elizabeth. The British Empire is also taught in schools in a largely positive light. Atwood also draws on her lived experience for details relating to the career of an entomologist – a job shared by both Atwood's father and Elaine's father. The level of detail in the novel, particularly relating to science, is a strength built on the back of memory and personal experience.

Memory is also important in the novel in relation to the characters' ability to recall details and events. Elaine often doubts her memory of Cordelia and finds herself wondering if things happened exactly the way she remembers them. Elaine's mother certainly misremembers Elaine's childhood when she talks to her adult daughter about how Grace and Carol – and not Cordelia – bullied Elaine. This is an example of the mind remembering what it wants to remember, and Elaine's mother undoubtedly takes comfort in imagining a version of events in which she did not completely ignore her daughter's suffering. In a similar vein, Cordelia seemingly manipulates her memory to her advantage. In high school, she mentions her childhood obsession with digging holes in her back garden, but seems to recall nothing of forcing Elaine to go into the hole and be semi-buried for an unspecified period of time. As this is one of Elaine's more traumatic memories from her time as Cordelia's victim, she stops seeing her friend shortly after this lapse of memory. It is unclear how intentional Cordelia's comments were, and if she truly does remember the incident. It is later implied that she does, as when Elaine refuses to help her escape the institution in which she is resident, she says, "I guess you've always hated me" (p. 405). Memories of bullying ultimately prove indelible.

CHRONOLOGY AND PERSPECTIVE

The novel is largely told through flashback from Elaine's perspective. Each new section of the novel generally begins with Elaine in present-day Toronto, going about her business in the days and hours leading up to her retrospective. The rest of the section then generally reverts to Elaine's past as told in the first person using the historical present. The use of the historical present means that the reader is often confronted with the opinions Elaine had at the time of the incident, rather than her retrospective opinions on the events of her childhood. In the chapters set in the present day, however, the reader does have access to Elaine's retrospective thoughts on her childhood and adolescence.

The non-linear chronology of the novel, by which Elaine's broadly chronological reminiscing about her past is interspersed with chapters set in the present day, allows for certain facts to be revealed at particularly impactful times. The most obvious example of this is the fate of Cordelia. The reader learns in Chapter 63, towards the end of the novel, that she was institutionalised due to her pill-taking habits. This adds tension to Elaine's expectation that she will attend the retrospective in the present day, which has been evident since the start of the novel. It also partly explains Elaine's wish to see her friend again: as well as wanting to catch up with her and to see if she is okay, she is also harbouring guilt at not visiting her again and, possibly, at not helping her leave the institution.

The non-linear chronology of the novel is used in other instances to create tension or to foreshadow events. For example, Stephen's death is briefly mentioned, almost as if in passing, in Chapter 56 when present-day Elaine thinks of him. His death is not described in the broadly chronological flashbacks of the novel, which tell the story of Elaine's life up to the retrospective, until Chapter 68. The two different time settings in the novel are also used to juxtapose the past with the present. This is perhaps most notable in Chapter 64 when Elaine, in the present day while married to her second husband Ben, has sex with her ex-husband Jon. The following chapter returns to her marriage to Jon and its dissolution. This is due to Jon's unfaithfulness, behaviour that Elaine is now repeating herself, in the role of the unfaithful spouse. This mirrors the way in which Elaine begins to torment Cordelia in high school, although never quite to the extent that Cordelia tormented her when they were children. In both instances Elaine switches from victim to instigator as she is shown to display behaviour that she herself has previously been hurt by.

FURTHER REFLECTION

SOME QUESTIONS TO THINK ABOUT...

- Why do you think Cordelia bullies Elaine?
- Discuss the growth of Elaine's character as the novel progresses.
- Why do you think Elaine has a relationship with Josef?
- Discuss the place of *Cat's Eye* in the Canadian literary canon. Is there anything that makes it specifically a Canadian novel?
- Compare *Cat's Eye* to another novel by Margaret Atwood you have read.
- Is *Cat's Eye* a feminist novel? Why/why not?
- Discuss the presentation of time in the novel.
- Given the many traits shared by both Elaine Risley and Margaret Atwood, can *Cat's Eye* be classed as an autobiographical novel or auto-fiction? Is there a difference between these two genres?

We want to hear from you!
Leave a comment on your online library
and share your favourite books on social media!

FURTHER READING

REFERENCE EDITION

- Atwood, M. (1988) *Cat's Eye*. London: Little, Brown.

MORE FROM
BRIGHTSUMMARIES.COM

- Reading guide – *Alias Grace* by Margaret Atwood.
- Reading guide – *The Blind Assassin* by Margaret Atwood.
- Reading guide – *The Handmaid's Tale* by Margaret Atwood.

Although the editor makes every effort to
verify the accuracy of the information published,
BrightSummaries.com accepts no responsibility for
the content of this book.

www.brightsummaries.com

Ebook EAN: 9782808019859

Paperback EAN: 9782808019866

Legal Deposit: D/2019/12603/157

Cover: © Primento

Digital conception by Primento, the digital partner of
publishers.

Printed in Great Britain
by Amazon